Barack Obama: Enraged at Israel

Roman Brackman

Library of Congress Cataloging-In-Publication data

Brackman, Roman

Brack Obama: Enraged at Israel / Roman Brackman

1. Obama, Barack. 2. Politics and Government: United States, 2008-2014

ISBN: 1-505-32219-7
ISBN-13: 978-1-505-32219-4

CONTENTS

ROMAN BRACKMAN

ACKNOWLEDGEMENTS

The author .would like to thank Michael Steinhardt for the many years of friendship and support. Also, special thanks to Alexander Gutkin – editor and publisher of many of my books for the last 10 years and running.

PREFACE

I have been gathering the information about Obama for a number of years.

In the course of this research, the article *"Obama and the Jews"* attracted my attention. It was published on October 24, 2008 in the *Chicago Jewish News*. It had a color photo of Obama wearing a white Jewish yarmulke and standing in front of a synagogue. The photo was accompanied by two captions. One of them read: *"On the eve of his historic nomination, a look at why some Jews love him and some don't trust him and at the key role Chicago Jews played in getting him to where he is."* The other caption, hovering over this photo, quoted Barack Obama, who in 2008 stated: *"Some of my earliest and most ardent supporters came from the Jewish community in Chicago."* One of Obama's "ardent supporters," Abner Mikva, a Chicago Congressman, Federal Judge and White House counsel to President Bill Clinton, was quoted in this article, stating: *"Clinton was the nation's first black president and I think when this is all over, people are going to say that Barack Obama is the first Jewish President."* This is why I decided to title my first Obama book *"First Jewish President."* It was published in 2012

"First Jewish President" by Roman Brackman

Most American Jews traditionally vote Democratic. In 1976 75% of them voted for Jimmy Carter and in 2008 75% of the Jewish vote went for Barack Obama.

In 2012 election only 68% of the Jewish vote went for Barack Obama. Some American Jews began to notice Obama's drift and the tension between Obama and Israeli Prime Minister Benjamin Netanyahu, who did not comply with Obama's insistence on Israeli concessions in the conflict with the Palestinians.

I wrote my book *"Barack Obama: Enraged at Israel,"* hoping to share with the readers my perception of Barack Obama the man and to try to point to the danger of his policies as well as to explain why he emerged from obscurity to be elected in 2008 and re-elected in 2012. Hugo Chaves' election and two re-elections had much to do with his promise to redistribute money to the people of Venezuela. Chaves had enough money from Venezuela oil deposits to buy votes. Barack Obama said that the United Sates have "no spending problem, only the revenue problem." He insists on raising taxes, because he needs "other people's money" to buy votes of people, who are increasingly dependent on the handouts from the entitlement and food stamps programs.

More insight about Obama comes from Wayne Allyn Root, Barack Obama's college classmate at Columbia University, class of '83. Wayne Allyn Root wrote:

Barrack Obama is no fool. He is not incompetent. To the contrary, he is brilliant. He knows exactly what he's doing. He is purposely overwhelming the U.S. economy to create systemic failure, economic crisis and social chaos - thereby destroying capitalism and our country from within. Barack Obama is my college classmate (Columbia University, class of '83). As Glenn Beck correctly predicted from day one, Obama is following the plan of Cloward & Piven, two professors at Columbia University. They outlined a plan to socialize America by overwhelming the system with government spending and entitlement demands. Add up the clues below. Taken individually they're alarming. Taken as a whole, it is a brilliant, Machiavellian game plan to turn the United States into a socialist/Marxist state with a permanent majority that desperately needs government for survival ... and can be counted on to always vote for bigger government. Why not? They have no responsibility to pay for it, universal health care. The health care bill had very little to do with health care. It had everything to do with unionizing millions of hospital and health care workers, as well as adding 15,000 to 20,000 new IRS agents (who will join government

5

employee unions). Obama doesn't care that giving free health care to 30 million Americans will add trillions to the national debt. What he does care about is that it cements the dependence of those 30 million voters to Democrats and big government. Who but a socialist revolutionary would pass this reckless spending bill in the middle of a depression?

All those public employees will vote loyally Democrat to protect their bloated salaries and pensions that are bankrupting America. The country goes broke, future generations face a bleak future, but Obama, the Democrat Party, government, and the unions grow more powerful. The ends justify the means. Raise taxes on small business owners, high-income earners, and job creators. Put the entire burden on only the top 20 percent of taxpayers, redistribute the income, punish success, and reward those who did nothing to deserve it (except vote for Obama). Reagan wanted to dramatically cut taxes in order to starve the government. Obama wants to dramatically raise taxes to starve his political opposition. With the acts outlined above, Obama and his regime have created a vast and rapidly expanding constituency of voters dependent on big government; a vast privileged class of public employees who work for big government; and a government dedicated to destroying capitalism and installing themselves as socialist rulers by overwhelming the system. Add it up and you've got the perfect Marxist scheme -- all devised by my Columbia University college classmate Barack Obama using the Cloward and Piven Plan.

DYSFUNCTIONAL FAMILY

Barack Obama's popularity drastically declined since he took office in 2009. Today, approximately 40% of the nation approve of his performance. Even in the early years of his presidency, he scared some people. Ben Stein, a very perceptive observer, in his article *"Our Angry President Scares Me,"* published in the December 2009 issue of NEWSMAX Magazine, quoted Phil De Muth, a "non-practicing psychologist of many years learning," as saying;

"It doesn't really matters what Obama's platform says or what he says or his handlers say. What matters is his unconscious agenda."

It is not important whether Obama's agenda is conscious *or* unconscious, but it is important to figure out what his agenda actually is. It is also important to know what he meant by promising to "fundamentally change America". Obama provided a clue by publishing his biography *"Dreams from My Father."* He titled it *"Dreams from My Father,"* not *"Dreams of My Father,"* which suggests, that Barack Obama identifies with his father and with his father's dreams. His father was Muslim and an admirer of the Soviet Union. He came to the United States from Kenya in the early sixties as an exchange student and met Obama's mother while both of them were attending Russian language coursed in a college. Obama's mother was one of the early hippies and also admired the Soviet Union. They married a few years before the Weather Underground terrorist William Ayers and his comrades were exploding bombs under American institutions and the anti-Vietnam war hippies gathered in Woodstock, smoking marihuana, denouncing "American war criminals" and shouting: *"Make Love, not war."* The student visa of Obama's father was canceled after the college administration complaint about his misconduct and he had to return to Kenya. Obama's mother also went to Kenya and lived for a while with Obama's father's family – his three wives, who resented and ill-treated her.

While writing my Carter book I was able to trace his roots to his many ancestors. In Barack Obama's case it proved very difficult to establish the truth. Donald Trump for a long time questioned validity of Obama's birth certificate which was released by the White House. Jerome R. Corsi, a Harvard Ph.D. is a WND senior staff reporter, who has authored many books, including No. 1 N.Y. Times best-sellers "The Obama Nation" and "Unfit for Command." Corsi's latest book is "Where's the REAL Birth Certificate?" in which he wrote:

Israel Hanukoglu, a former science adviser to Israeli Prime Minister Benjamin Netanyahu, Ph.D. an award-winning researcher, a professor of biochemistry and molecular biology in the Department of Molecular Biology at Ariel University Center of Samaria, established that the White House's release of the Obama document in April 2011, after years of controversy, "raised in our minds the possibility that there could be something suspicious about the information available on this document." The publication "of such a blatantly fake document about something as basic as the birthplace of Mr. Obama, should raise great concern about the suitability of the person who is holding the reins on the most powerful country of the World

What we know is that after Kenya, Ann Dunham returned to America and named her son Barack Hussein Obama.

Later on she married Lolo Soetoro, an exchange student from Indonesia, a Muslim, and they went to Indonesia. For several years she lived with her new husband and son in this Muslim country, but than returned to America with her son. Barack Obama's father died in Kenya in a car accident. While **Obama** lived in Indonesia, a Muslim country, he learned to recite prayers from Koran in perfect Arabic. Google search reveals this photo:

The Soetoro family in Indonesia - 1970

L to R, Lolo Soetoro, Stanley Ann Dunham Soetoro, baby Maya Soetoro, and 9 year old Barry Soetoro (aka Barack Hussein Obama) Bellow is Indonesian school registration document, released on January 24, 2007, by the Fransiskus Assisi school in Jakarta, Indonesia, shows the registration of Barack Obama under the name Barry Soetoro made by his step-father, Lolo Soetoro.

Bellow is the official translation to English of Indonesian school record. On this document the phrase: Tempat dan tanggal lahir, located near the top left side, has Honolulu listed as the place of birth.

Obama's Indonesian school record

So, even back then, the parents we're saying he was born in Hawaii.

This document states:

Name: Barry Soetoro

Religion: Islam

Nationality: Indonesian

David Mendell in his biography of Barack Obama wrote about Obama's life as a "secret smoker" and how he "went to great lengths to conceal the habit." He also wrote that Obama's childhood mentor, Frank Marshall Davis, was a communist. Obama, in his book, "*Dreams from My Father*," refers to him repeatedly as just "Frank." In this book Obama admits attending "socialist conferences" and coming into contact with Marxist literature. Frank Marshall Davis was publicly identified as a member of the Communist Party USA (CPUSA), a party subservient to the Soviet Union. Obama was listening Davis' "poetry" and got Davis' advice on his career path. It was in Chicago that Obama became a "community organizer" and came into contact with the Democratic Socialists of America, which maintains close ties to European socialist groups and parties through the Socialist International (SI). Obama also came into contact with William Ayers and Carl Davidson, two former members of the Students for a Democratic Society (SDS). The SDS laid siege to college campuses across America in the 1960s, mostly in order to protest the Vietnam War, and spawned the terrorist Weather Underground organization. William Ayers was a member of the Weather Underground and is now a college professor who served with Obama on the board of the Woods Fund of Chicago. Davidson is now a figure in the Committees of Correspondence for Democracy and Socialism, an offshoot of the old Moscow-controlled CPUSA. He helped organize the 2002 rally where Obama came out against the Iraq War. Professor Gerald Horne, a contributing editor of the Communist Party journal *Political Affairs*, <u>wrote</u>:

"Obama's victory was more than a progressive move; it was a dialectical leap ushering in a qualitatively new era of struggle. Marx once compared revolutionary struggle with the work of the mole, which sometimes burrows so far beneath the ground that he leaves no trace of his movement on the surface. This is the old revolutionary 'mole,' not only showing his traces on the surface but also breaking through."

OBAMA AND CARTER

Several scandals rocked the Barack Obama presidency during his second term in office. The Benghazi disaster, the IRS scandal, the denial of services to American wars veterans, the release from Guantanamo of five top Al-Qaida commanders in exchange for an alleged American army deserter. Then there was the sudden incursion of illegal children from South America. They were encouraged to cross our borders by Obama's peddling of "comprehensive immigration reform" which was interpreted as *permissimo* (permission) to obtain legal status in America. These scandals have been in the news almost daily, but these scandals pale into insignificance by comparison to the looming conquest of Iraq and Syria by the ISIS, the most dangerous terrorist army, which occupied large parts of these countries, but Obama announced:

"All options are on the table."

One option has not been on the table. Obama has insisted that "American boots will not be on the ground." This "politically correct" mantra convinced leaders of ISIS that with America "leading from behind," no other nation will put its soldiers to fight in this war without American troops on the ground. The leaders of ISIS became convinced and that they can continue their conquest with impunity. The victorious march of ISIS also incites the mentally disturbed people in America, Canada and Australia to avenge heir imaginary grievances. They jump on the fast moving ISIS bandwagon. This multiplies converts to Islam, motivating them to murder innocent people with hatchets, knives and guns. "No American boots on the ground" declarations have been Obama's major provocation. I was tempted to title my Obama book "Barack Obama Provocateur - in- Chief," but I had earlier used a similar title for my Carter book "Jimmy Carter Provocateur-in-Chief." Dr. Sam Vaknin, who published many books and articles on narcissism, in his letter to me wrote: *"There are so many similarities between these two Democratic Presidents, it is positively unnerving!"* In 1980 I published my book "Jimmy Carter Provocateur-in-Chief." In the Author's Note I wrote:

Soon after the 1976 Presidential election, the American press reported that Soviet representatives had been nervously asking around in Washington circles: "What kind of a man is Carter? He must be either naive or a provocateur!" That question and the two choices did not surprise me. The Russian mind was at work; the frame of reference was familiar. I was born in Moscow and lived there for some thirty years before coming to this country. We all remain prisoners of our pasts. I was asking the same question early in the 1976 campaign, and my vision of Carter vacillated between those two alternatives. I could not explain otherwise his sudden emergence from obscurity, his strange insistence on being an "outsider," the almost palpable shallowness of his personality, his ever-oncoming twitchy smile. I was struck by his peculiar glibness, by the amazing ease with which he juggled his positions on various issues and by his crafty manipulation of the national traumas of Vietnam and Watergate. I watched his T.V. performance and read his campaign autobiography "Why Not the Best?" I followed his statements and searched for clues in the press. Various articles referred to Carter as an enigma, mystery and a riddle. His pronouncements were described as confusing. He was accused of sending mixed signal rich in "symbolism but devoid of substance." Some articles pointed to his "weird performance" but offered no explanations. To the American mind the choice also split into two extremes. Carter was a deeply religious and honest man or he was a con-artist and double crosser. Time magazine reported that a sixteen-year-old California girl, Melanie Field, after watching one of Carter's televised campaign appearances, turned to her father and asked: "Dad is Jimmy Carter a weirdo?" Dad's response was not reported. When I came across this story, the various American interpretations of Carter proved inadequate. To me, the Russian label provocateur was, unfortunately, the answer. A con-artist or double crosser connoted a small-time operator, while a provocateur was capable of causing national and global upheavals by instigating conflicts. The girl's unanswered question haunted me. To me she personified a bewildered America in danger. I felt that if I had the answer, she deserved to have it too. I promptly wrote an article, "Behind Carter's Twitchy Smile," and sent copies to several magazines. I received polite notes of rejection. Behind the politeness I sensed incredulity. I realized that my vision of Carter as a provocateur was threatening and foreign to American tradition. Besides, early in 1976, there was no record of Carter's presidency to substantiate my frightening view of him. The tendency to dismiss my perception and to blot it out altogether was strong in me too.

Even as a boy I had a dream of escaping from Russia and coming to America, my wonderland. My childhood belonged to the time of Stalin's Great Purges, which claimed many of my close relatives. Fear and alienation from Soviet life poisoned my entire adolescence. I dreaded airing my "anti-Soviet views," but could not help expressing them. Informers denounced me and my intimate friends. The secret police listened in and taped our conversation. In 1949, when I was eighteen, I and my two friends and classmates Mikhail Margulis and Vitaly Svechinsky attempted an escape across the Soviet-Turkish border. We naively fancied it was possible. We failed and were arrested. For almost a year the Secret Police questioned us in the Lubyanka and Butyrki prisons, trying to prove to us that we were "American and Zionist agents," but they could not cite a single instance of our contact with foreigners, because we had never even seen one. Our only link with the "other world" was an occasional word reaching us from the heavily jammed radio broadcasts of "Voice of America." Each of us got away with "childish prison sentences" (by Soviet standards) of ten years imprisonment in various political strict regime camps for an "attempt to betray the motherland, anti-Soviet propaganda and agitation and belonging to an anti-Soviet organization" which actually consisted of three teenagers. I was sent to Norilsk in the polar region of Siberia and my two friends to similar places in Magadan and Pot'ma. Stalin's death in 1953 saved us. Along with millions of prisoners we were set free in the first post-Stalin amnesty, having served only half our sentence. Four years later, my family and I managed to sneak from Moscow to Poland. Three years later, in 1962, we arrived in America. I became a citizen in the 1968 and cast my first vote in the 1968 Presidential election.

Carter's record of the last four years has reinforced my early sense of him. I do not mean the record of galloping inflation, rising unemployment and deepening recession. These problems are dwarfed by the prospect of a Soviet-American confrontation escalating into a nuclear war. Initially I had wondered whether Carter's conflicting foreign policy pronouncements had stemmed from naiveté or were deliberate provocations. I had wanted to convince myself that Carter was an incompetent man who meant well. I resisted my growing awareness of him as a provocateur whose defective personality, consciously or not, drove him to promote instability, setting the stage for a military conflict, and conditioning Americans and the world for a state of irreversible belligerence. I could not believe that America would tolerate and support such a President. I asked myself again and again whether my Russian background, my study of Russian history, and the book I had been writing on Stalin influenced my appraisal of Carter. After all, Russians have been particularly oversensitive to the type of provocateur Dostoyevsky immortalized in Peter Verkhovensky, a hero of The Possessed. Foreign scholars also came to recognize the tragic role of the "possessed souls" in Russia's upheavals. The late Bertram D. Wolfe wrote that there was "something in the Russian temperament and scene that engendered these men of ambivalent spirit and double role." The Soviet historian Roy Medvedev described Stalin as a "typical provocateur, whose purges and show trials of the thirties were beyond doubt one of the most monstrous provocations in history." Did I succeed during my new life in America in freeing myself from this Russian "temperament and scene" to be able to see Carter for what he was, instead of fitting him into my distinctly Russian experience? I do not pretend to be completely liberated from my Russian past. Without it my insight into Carter's mind probably would not have occurred.

The Soviet leaders have examined Carter's record. As Stalin's heirs and pupils, as beneficiaries of his Great Purges, they can spot a provocateur when they see one. But they also may confuse naiveté with provocation. That they accuse Carter of provocations means nothing. It is common to see another in the image of one's own self. The Soviets have routinely projected their own provocative tactics on chosen scapegoats. They are masters at fishing in troubled waters. They incite conflicts, finance "revolutions," spur terrorist groups and wage proxy wars. In the past, my inclination was to dismiss Soviet accusations as mere reflections of their own bad conscience. Admittedly the difference between naiveté and provocation, in practical terms, is not easily discernible. I will never forget a man who taught me a lesson in telling the difference between naiveté and provocation. Yakov Abramovich Tsynman was about fifty and I barely twenty, when we met in the Norilsk prison camp in 1951. He had joined the Bolsheviks on the eve of the Russian Revolution, fought in the Civil War and later joined the Soviet Secret Police, rising rapidly in the ranks, reaching the position of the Assistant Chief of the Azerbaijan NKVD (Secret Police). Arrested in the late thirties, he was one of the rare survivors of the Great Purges by the time I wound up in the camp. Several inmates advised me to avoid him because of his secret police past. They also told me he was a provocateur, who by extolling the Soviet system and praising Stalin, induced others to contradict him and then reported their comments to the authorities.

I came to realize that Tsynman was a true Communist believer, one of those decent, but naive idealists who mistook dogma for reality. I asked him how it could be that after having spent more than thirteen years in prison camps and having witnessed and experienced the ultimate misery and brutality of the Soviet system, he still refused to recognize its evil. He used to offer various justifications, praise Stalin's "genius" and proclaim that the Soviet system was the most advanced and human, and that it would eventually fulfill every promise. He was a kind and compassionate man with big blue eyes. He never denounced me. In the winter of 1952, while crossing railroad tracks with a bundle of shovels and picks on his shoulder, he was crushed between two freight cars when a locomotive suddenly shoved them together. Friends asked me to notify his family. I smuggled out a letter to his wife and two daughters with the tragic message through a friendly guard. Even while in Russia my strong tendency was to see naiveté instead of its look-alike provocation. This is especially true now that my faith in America has come into conflict with my perception of its President. I struggled to dismiss Soviet accusations as groundless, but Carter's record has forced me, against my life-long inclination, to feel certain sympathy for the Soviet predicament in dealing with Carter. A high State Department official, puzzled by Carter's conflicting policies, observed, "There's probably a method to the madness. I confess all I see is the madness." Carter's method is no mystery to me, and, I surmise, the Soviets recognize it too. Carter has a deep emotional need to be "the most powerful man in the world," as the advertisement of his inaugural medal describes him. Edmund Muskie said that Carter was tying the hostage crisis to his primary campaign. Has Carter timed his provocations to suit his reelection campaign? If so, will the peak of tension coincide with the eve of the election? Could Carter ignite a global conflict to avoid defeat? I think the Soviets have been asking these questions and their recent military activities, especially their invasion of Afghanistan, suggest that they are getting ready for this high risk period. Around the time the Soviets began to wonder whether Carter was naive or a provocateur, they sent an agent to Plains, Georgia, to interview Miss Lillian, Carter's mother. Miss Lillian later said that she "took good care" of this agent who "was only interested in Jimmy as a boy." Publication of Carter's childhood biography was not on the Soviet mind. They were digging at the roots of Carter's emotional life to verify their growing awareness of him as a provocateur out of control. They were on the right track. Beginning with Carter's roots, I invite the reader to follow me to a vision that is scary. One major barrier has to be overcome - the natural resistance to accepting something immensely disturbing, which may tempt my reader, as it did me, to explain the vision away. Arguments for that are readily available. America with her strong political and humanist traditions could not possibly have fallen for a dangerous provocateur. Even if she did, the free press and constitutional safeguards would surely stop him from dragging the country and the world into the abyss. That, I hope, proves to be true, but only if Carter is recognized for what he is. That is the reason I wrote this book.

In Chapter 6 - *"I'd Rather Commit Suicide, Political or Otherwise, Than Hurt Israel"* I wrote about Carter's Middle East policy, which became Israel's nightmare during his presidency. For years Carter persisted in bashing Israel even after his defeat in the 1980 presidential elections. In Chapter 7 - *"The 54th Hostage"* I wrote about Carter's role in provoking the downfall of the Iranian Shah. I quoted Rowland Evans and Robert

Novak article *"Did Carter Send a General to Hasten the Shah's fall?"* which was published in the *New York Post* on November 26, 1979. Rowland Evans and Robert Novak quoted General Alexander Haig, who had "accused the Carter Administration of assigning General Hoyer, Haig's deputy, to hasten the Shah's fall," stating that General Haig "had not gone public with his sensational charge," but what he had told privately, was confirmed in the Pentagon records, which showed that the Chairman of the Joint Chiefs, General David Jones, had called Haig in December 1978 "to inform him that President Carter wished to send Huyser to Teheran for meetings with Iranian military leaders. Haig had asked whether the purpose of Huyser's mission was to urge the Generals to re-establish law and order, or to tell the Shah to leave the country." Haig's response was:

"I do not concur. It is wrong to use a professional military man to execute a political mission; if dirty work was in the offing, a political emissary was more appropriate. An attempt by the United States to force the Shah out would lead to disaster in Iran."

Rowland Evans and Robert Novak wrote that Charles Duncan, then the Deputy Secretary of Defense, discussed Haig's reservations with the Joint Chiefs (Defense Secretary Harold Brown was in California) and took the matter to Carter and Zbigniew Brzezinski and that Carter told Duncan "to overrule Haig and to cut the orders for the Huyser mission to Teheran" They wrote that Duncan had said, "the purpose of the Huyser mission was to cause the military in Iran to have confidence in U.S. support and to avoid disintegration of the military." Duncan acknowledged that "the military did ultimately decide not to resist Ayatollah Khomeini." According to the article, "Haig has not taken seriously Duncan's explanation and regarded it as a 'smoke-screen' and believed that Huyser was an instrument of Carter's policy to drop the Shah." The Shah's own memoirs, according to excerpts published in the December 1979 issue of the London magazine *Now!*, left no doubt about his interpretation of the Huyser mission. The Shah's own memoirs left no doubt about his interpretation of the Houser mission. According to the excerpts published in the December 1979 issue of the London magazine "Now!" where the Shah is quoted as saying:

"At the beginning of January 1978, when I was still on the throne of Iran, Huyser arrived secretly in Teheran with the clear purpose of 'neutralizing' the Iranian Army and preventing it from fighting the Khomeini mobs. When I received Huyser and Ambassador William H. Sullivan, I realized that the one thing that was on the minds of both men was to know on what day and at what time I should be leaving."

On January 16, 1978 the Shah left Teheran and on February 11 Khomeini took over and started mass executions, in which all the Generals, whom Huyser had "neutralized," perished. General Huyser was appointed the Chief of the United States Military Airlift Command at Scott Air Force Base in Illinois. He refused to comment on either the newspapers' reports, or the Shah's memoirs, saying through his spokesman that any statement by him could be "counterproductive to our national effort."

I ended the final chapter "Commander–in–Chief Jimmy Carter" with the following observation:

I doubt that Carter would consult Congress or anybody before going down in flames and dragging humanity along with him. I have a horrible vision: 140 million escapees stampeding on the way to the George Washington Bridge and other specified routes, while our American Peter Verkhovensky (the hero in Dostoyevsky's book "The Possessed") takes to 'the hills' or takes off in his 'Doomsday plane,' leaving behind the 'burning towns' with 'crazed people.' And Barbara Walter's plea, 'be wise with us ... be good to us' does not ring in his ears.

William Loeb, President and Publisher of Manchester Union-Leader wrote a remarkable letter in response to my article *"Behind Carter's Twitchy Smile"*. Below is his letter:

November 5, 1976

Dear Mr. Brackman;

Thank you very much indeed for your piece on Jimmy Carter. Unfortunately, it came in while I was out of the country and came to my attention too late to run before the election. May I say that you have analyzed Carter very accurately, in my opinion? Mrs. Loeb and I had lunch with him about a year ago with just one other person present, just the four of us. I think that he was very well informed regarding my stance on various issues, but on the surface he was thoroughly in agreement with me. But I was watching his eyes, and afterwards, I said to Mrs. Loeb what I thought, and she said, "That is the most untrustworthy character I ever did see!" To which I could only add, "Amen!" He is a very dangerous individual in my opinion. I think the question asked by the little girl and the punch line of this story is quite correct. I am not, of course, a psychiatrist, but my observation is that this is the type of neurotic person who drives himself beyond his capacity, like Adolf Hitler and others of this ilk who are extremely determined to succeed at any cost, and are without any moral restraint whatsoever. Knowing Admiral Rickover, I wrote him on the subject of his association with Carter. Also knowing him, I expected exactly what happened. He called me and we talked for twenty minutes or so, and he never let me know how he really felt about Carter. The obvious implication of this is that if Carter had been all that he, Carter, said he was Rickover would not have hesitated in saying so. The fact Rickover would say nothing one way or the other tells me the whole story: Carter was not much, but that Rickover wasn't sure that he, Carter, would be our next President, and so he, Rickover, better be careful of what he said. Carter's rise to the White House has that strange unhealthy quality about it that Adolf Hitler's rise to the Commander of the Third Reich had—improbable, but made possible by the tangled times and tremendous drive on the part of the individual. Carter's mother made another remark that Mrs. Loeb picked up that you don't mention in your article, namely, that Jimmy is like a little baby with steel claws. Your description of Carter's inability to accept a loss, as well as the way he reacts to it, is another example of lack of balance. Yours is really one of the best pieces on Carter I have ever read. I wish it could have been printed in some of the national magazines with wide circulation before the election. It might have awakened some people. The part dealing with Jimmy telling his audience: "If you have any questions or advice for me, please write. Just put 'Jimmy Carter, Plains, Georgia' on the envelope, and I'll get it. I open every letter myself and read them all" Boy! What a liar! I just think it is so tragic that the American public should have fallen for such a double-crossing hypocrite. By the way, what are you doing now to keep the wolf away from the door?

Very sincerely,

William Loeb, President

In June 1979 Ronald Reagan was scheduled to address a campaign rally in New Haven. I went to this rally with the intention of giving my Carter book to him. I sat on a bench, waiting for Reagan to come. A man, whom I did not know, set next to me and asked what I was doing at the rally. I understood that he was a Secret Service agent and told him that I wanted to give my book to Reagan. "May I see your book?" he asked and I gave it to him. He read the title, looked at a couple of pages, wished me good luck and left. He probably thought that I was some kind of a nut, but not a dangerous nut, and decided to leave me alone. I stood in the crowd when Ronald and Nancy Reagan were passing by. Because Nancy Reagan walked close to me and Ronald Reagan was further away, I gave my Carter book to her. I have no idea whether she or he ever bothered to read my Carter book. I sent this book to a number of book stores. Except for one review by a radio commentator, the book did not have any publicity. I was not aware of any reaction to this book.

2009: WHY HOLOCAUST SHOCKED OBAMA'S UNCLE

Rafael Medoff in his Jun 5, 2009 article *"Why Holocaust shocked Obama's uncle[1]"* wrote:

President Barack Obama's planned visit to the former Nazi concentration camp of Buchenwald on June 5 will have special significance because his great uncle, Charlie Payne, was one of the American soldiers who liberated a sub-camp of Buchenwald sixty-four years ago.

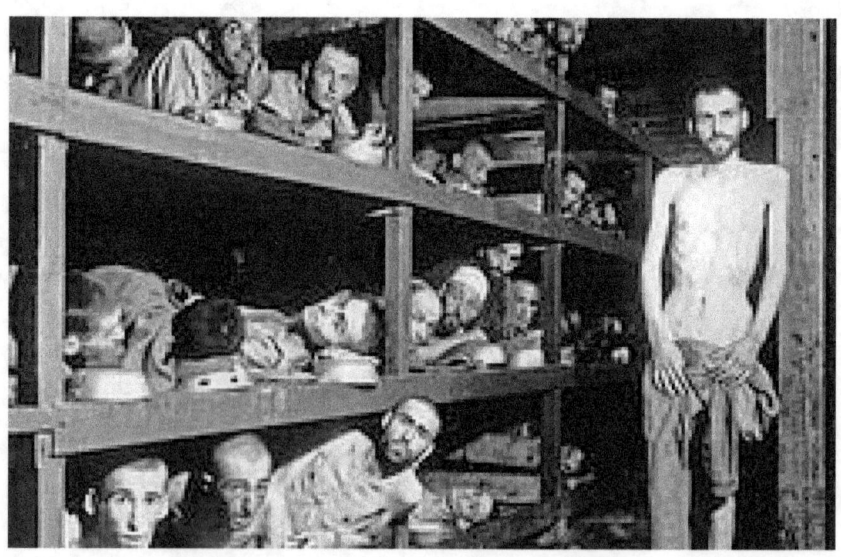

In this April 16, 1945 Buchenwald inmates are seen inside their barracks a few days after US troops liberated the concentration camp near Weimar. Photo: AP

On April 4, 1945, Payne's unit came across the sub-camp, called Ohrdruf, as they chased the retreating German army. The Nazi guards

---

[1] Jerusalem Post 06/05/2009, Op-Ed "Why Holocaust shocked Obama's uncle"

had already abandoned the camp and forced most of the prisoners to take part in a death march. They left behind piles of emaciated corpses. Ohrdruf was the first Nazi *concentration camp* that the American army encountered, and it was there, eight days later, that General Dwight Eisenhower saw the disturbing sights that prompted him to invite journalists and Members of Congress to view the evidence of Nazi atrocities first hand. "The things I saw beggar description," he wrote. "The visual evidence and the verbal testimony of starvation, cruelty and bestiality were so overpowering as to leave me a bit sick."

Then-candidate Obama spoke of his great-uncle on the presidential campaign trail last year. Urging increased funding for treatment of post-traumatic stress disorder among soldiers, Obama said that when Charlie returned home, "he just went up into the attic and he didn't leave the house for six months. Now obviously something had really affected him deeply, but at that time, there just weren't the kinds of facilities to help somebody work through that kind of pain." The horror that Charlie and his fellow-GIs felt upon seeing the Nazis' victims was compounded by the fact that they were completely unprepared for what they were about to see. Although the army's senior brass was fully informed about the Nazis' mass murder of millions of European Jews, ordinary soldiers were never told what they were likely to see as they made their way through formerly Axis-controlled territory. "A concentration camp at Dachau was a complete surprise to all of us," recalled Col. Walter J. Fellenz, a commander of the First Battalion, which was involved in liberating that camp. Likewise George Oiye, of the 522nd Field Artillery Battalion: "We were not ordered to take Dachau; we just kind of stumbled on to it. I didn't even know it existed." Staff Sgt. Johnnie Stevens of the 761st Tank Battalion, which helped liberate Gunskirchen, a sub-camp of Mauthausen, said: "At the time, we did not know those camps existed. Our government lied to us. We were not prepared for what we found." Army publications were no help. Consider the experience of Sgt. Richard Paul, a reporter for Yank, an army magazine for soldiers. In October 1944 - six months before Obama's great-uncle entered

Ohrdruf - Sgt. Paul submitted an article about the mass murder of the Jews in Auschwitz, the editors of Yank turned it down, saying it was "too Semitic." They told him to rewrite it so that it "did not deal principally with Jews."

The army's other magazine, Stars and Stripes, was no different. It was not until April 1945 that Stars and Stripes finally published article about Nazi atrocities and concentration camps, and even then, the articles did not mention Jews. The average GI reading Stars and Strips had no way of knowing that Jews were the main victims of the Nazis. The line followed by Yank and Stars and Stripes was unfortunately consistent with the approach of the Roosevelt administration as a whole. Calling attention to the fact that the Jews were being singled out for persecution would have increased pressure on the US government to grant them refuge - something President Franklin Roosevelt did not want to do. The chiefs of the US Office of War Information instructed their staff that coverage of the Nazi mass-murders would be "confused and misleading if it appears to be simply affecting the Jewish people." A meeting of the American, British, and Soviet foreign ministers in Moscow in October 1943 issued a statement threatening postwar punishment for Nazi war crimes against conquered populations. It mentioned "French, Dutch, Belgian or Norwegian hostages ...Cretan peasants ... the people of Poland" but not Jews. In a similar spirit, General Eisenhower himself removed all references to Jews from a leaflet the Allies air-dropped over Europe in September 1944, threatening to punish anyone who collaborated in Nazi atrocities against civilians. Even President Roosevelt's 1944 message commemorating the first anniversary of the Warsaw Ghetto revolt - a rebellion by Jewish fighters - did not mention the Jews. Arthur Szyk, the famous artist and Holocaust rescue activist, remarked bitterly that Europe's Jews were being "treated as a pornographically subject you cannot discuss it in polite society." On several recent occasions, President Obama expressed regrets about some past US policies and their impact abroad. Perhaps, his visit to Buchenwald, and his memories of what happened to his great-uncle, will inspire the president to say a few words about the Roosevelt administration's appalling policy toward Europe's Jews during the Holocaust and about the lessons to be learned, in order to help stop genocide today.

On Friday, May 29, 2009 Newsmax_magazine posted article "MAD-AS-HELL – Obama using Buchenwald for Political Purpose:

Barack Obama's great uncle Charles Payne offered some blunt language as to why his nephew is visiting the memorial at the former Buchenwald concentration camp next week during his trip to Europe and the Middle East. Charles Payne said;

"This is a trip that he chose, not because of me I'm sure, but for political reasons," Charles Payne told the German magazine Spiegel. "Perhaps his visit also has something to do with improving his standing with (German Chancellor) Angela Merkel. She gave him a hard time during his campaign and also afterwards. I know there was some talk about how Obama fudged this but was there ever any reporting about how his Uncle stated that Obama never talked or asked him about his WW2 experience? Is this just another example of how the media just decided to let Obama have a free pass because they wanted him as President and didn't want to anything to derail him? I was quite surprised when the whole thing came up and Barack talked about my war experiences in Nazi Germany, We had never talked about that before. Of course it came out immediately that he was wrong since there are enough people in America who know that Auschwitz is in the East and that the camp was liberated by the Red Army."

OBAMA'S SLINGSHOT

Aaron David Miller, a Middle East analyst, author, and a member of the U.S. Advisory Council of Israel Policy Forum, in his article "Wooing the gods of the peace process" wrote[2]:

The Obama administration's inability to resist temptation to bridge the gaps on Jerusalem, borders, security, and the fate of Palestinian refugees, Obama might end up in another make or break summit…This is particularly important for Obama who, much like Bill Clinton believes that through the force of his personality, he can act as a transformative agent in international politics."

At the end of his article Miller sums up his argument by stating:

And in failing Obama will be hanging a 'closed for the season' sign on American efforts in Arab-Israeli peacemaking. And far from being the architect of a negotiated two-state solution, Obama will end up being the American president whose administration presided over its demise.

The key words here are "force of his personality" and "inability to resist temptation." These words and Obama's record make Miller's prediction plausible.

Barak Obama served as a "community organizer" in Chicago. For

---

[2] Foreign Policy, 12/20/2010, "Wooing the gods of the peace process"

twenty years he attended Rev. Jeremiah Wright's Church. Then he served one term in Illinois State Senate and half term in U.S. Senate. Thereafter, Barak Obama's smooth talking catapulted him straight into the White House. At the start of his campaign Obama declared his intention to stop the Iraq War at once, but then said that he intends to withdraw our troops in 16 months. He accused John McCain of running for "Bush third term" while the talking heads in the media proclaimed "failures" of Bush's policies. Bob Herbert in his Op-Ed article wrote:

"Anger at George W. Bush is white-hot." (NYT, August 26, p.19)

History has many examples of leaders who failed to deliver on a silver platter a quick and glorious victory to their people who felt "white-hot" anger and demanded a change. The media denounced "failures" of Bush's policies and Obama won the 2008 presidential election, running actually not against John McCain, a Vietnam War hero, but against George Bush, who failed to deliver on a silver platter a quick and glorious victory and inspired "white-hot" anger of people who wanted a change. During the long Korean War Harry Truman had even lower rating than George Bush had at the end of his term. The German and Russian people were» white-hot" angry during the protracted WW1. The German Emperor was exiled and the Russian Tsar and his entire family were murdered. The German people got Hitler's fascism and Russian people got Lenin's and Stalin's communism. French history offers another example of "change." Dissatisfied with protracted wars and taxation, the Paris mob on July 14, 1789 stormed Bastille prison, freeing seven common criminals, among them Marquis de Sade, the infamous sadist, who shouted to the enraged mob: "They are killing the prisoners here!" which caused a riot. King Louis XVI was guillotined and Marie-Antoinette met the same fate. Their son, the Dauphin, was tortured and died in prison. Napoleon became the Emperor of France. Hitler the Fuhrer, Stalin the Vozhd and Napoleon the Emperor had sprung up from nowhere.

Obama made "change" the battle cry of his campaign. Because of the obvious success of the surge in Iraq, Obama stopped talking about the war, folded the white flag of surrender and jumped instead on the tidal wave of economic tsunami which carried him into the White House. The voting public did not realize that this tsunami had its origin in the "spread the wealth" ideology of the Obama-type of "community organizers" and their ideological allies in the Congress, who intimidated American banks into lending mortgages to people, who could not afford them and allowing the banks to package these bad mortgages together with he good ones into "mortgage-backed securities" to be traded on international stock markets. These fraudulent "mortgage-backed securities" became the poison pills that almost killed the world financial system. Now Obama claims that his "stimulus" bailout of billions of dollars has saved America from economic collapse. But the economy shows little improvements. His Medicare reform has run into stiff resistance of people in the town hall meetings and in Congress. His once soaring popularity plummeted. In his biography Obama told that once as he walked with his grandmother, a "typical white person," who had made a derogatory remark about a black man, who was passing them by, and he "cringed." When it was reported that a Boston policeman had arrested a black professor, Obama, after admitting that he did not know the circumstances of this arrest, "cringed" and called this policeman "stupid." Obama did not apologize, but said that he had poorly "calibrated" his words and then tried to drown the controversy in bottles of bear at the White House "bear summit."

Obama tried to outpromise Hillary Clinton who in her speech at the American-Israeli Public Affairs Committee (AIPAC) had said: "I would obliterate Iran if Israel was attacked. » Obama in his speech at AIPAC declared: "Security of Israel is sacrosanct and if Iran attacks Israel, I will use any means, I mean, any means, to defend Israel." In his lapel Obama wore an Israeli flag. Obama also said: "Jerusalem will remain the capital of Israel and it must remain undivided." But he immediately took back his words, saying that they were "badly phrased" and were "an example where we had some poor phrasing" and "clarified" his comments, saying: "Jerusalem is a final status issue, which means its status, has to be negotiated between the two parties." Obama revealed his sympathy toward one of the parties - the Palestinians. He said: "Nobody is suffering more than Palestinian people. That is why I hope for loosening up aid restrictions to the Palestinian people." In a closed-door meeting with several members of Cleveland's Jewish community on February 25, 2008 Obama said:

"I think there is a strain within the pro-Israel community that says unless you adopt pro-Likud approach to Israel, then you're anti-Israel, and that can't be the measure of our friendship with Israel."

Obama's "measure of our friendship with Israel" was revealed after the election of Benjamin Netanyahu, who as Israel's Prime Minister heads the Likud led coalition in the Knesset. The Washington Post Editorial stated:

"US provoked Israeli public rallying for Netanyahu, because of the one sided demand for Israeli concessions on settlement issue."

Thomas Friedman in his OP-Ed article "Free Marriage Counseling" stated:

"Bottom line: Israelis need to understand this is no longer the Bush administration anymore, where they had a run of the White House; they have a real problem with America on settlements."

Friedman proceeds to teach Obama how to get tough on Israel as if Obama needed his advice. Friedman also quoted the left-leaning Israeli newspaper Ha'arez, which had accused Netanyahu of calling "two Obama aids pushing the freeze on settlement as self-hating Jews working out their identity crisis by working over Israel." Rev. Jeremiah Wright complained:

"Them Jews do not let me talk to Obama!"

By "them Jew" Rev. Jeremiah Wright meant David Axelrod and Rohm Emanuel, both of whom are Jewish. Axelrod and Emanuel, as well other "progressive" Jews are self-admiring Jews, working out their identity crisis by working over Israel. They proudly parade their "progressive" ideology and advertise their "objectivity and evenhandedness" in the Arab-Israeli conflict. Friedman also stated:

"For the last 40 years, a succession of Israeli governments has misled, manipulated or persuaded naïve U.S. Presidents, creating a huge moral, security and economic burden for Israel and its friends."

Friedman, judging by his last name, is apparently Jewish. He counts himself among those who care about Israel. He is sick of the naiveté of the former U.S. Presidents, including George W. Bush. Friedman is also sick of the pro-Israel Jews who, as he put it, "had a run of the Bush White House."

Obama invited leaders of the "progressive" Jewish organizations to the White House. M.J. Rosenberg, a spokesman for the Israel Policy

Forum, a left-leaning Jewish group, stated:

"Obama understands that he is going to get more support from the Americans for Peace Now, the J-Street Jews and Israel Policy Forum than from the more mainstream Jewish organizations. He appeals to groups like J-Street because we're his natural base of support."

Jeremy Ben-Ami, the Executive Director of the J-Street left-leaning Jewish group stated:

"We're really pleased to be included in the White House meeting. The voice that we bring of pro-Israel, pro-peace Jews and other friends of Israel is extremely important to hear to understand the diversity of views in the Jewish community."

But Mort Klein of the Zionist Organization of America complained that his organization had not been invited to the White House meeting and stated:

"Obama had said publicly that he wants to hear all different views. Obama reached out to Iranian President Mahmud Ahmadinejad and Venezuelan President Hugo Chavez. When it comes to Israel, he's not that interested in hearing views that are different from his."

The Smith Research poll taken in August 2009 on behalf of The Jerusalem Post found that only 4% of Israelis see US President Barack Obama's policies as pro-Israel and believe that he is pro-Palestinian. Israelis voted for Netanyahu because the antennas in their *pupiks* (Yiddish for belly buttons) signaled danger to them in Obama's "approach" to Israel. It has been reported that Obama plans to meet Benjamin Netanyahu and Mahmud Abbas to revitalize the "peace process." No doubt, Obama counts on his ability to charm both of them to follow hid guidance. In his much advertised Cairo speech Obama extended his hand to the Muslim and Arab world, proudly mentioned his name Barak Hussein Obama, pointing to his years of living in the Muslim countries. In this speech he also mentioned Israel as the "Jewish homeland," omitting the fact that that Israel is the Jewish state. This omission was not accidental. Nothing what Obama says or neglects to say, has been accidental. It has been repeated at nausea by the media that Abbas is Israel's "moderate partner." Obama said "Jewish homeland" to please the Palestinian President Mahmud Abbas who recently had declared;

"You could call this land Israel or whatever you want, but I and Palestinians will never recognize it as a Jewish state."

Anne Bayefsky, a senior fellow at the Hudson Institute, in her article "Obama's stunning offence to Israel and the Jewish people" pointed to Obama's Cairo speech in which he equated the Holocaust of six million Jews to Palestinian "dislocation" and suffering of "Palestinian people in pursuit of a homeland." Obama equated their "daily humiliation… that comes with occupation" with "segregation of black slaves in America" and "people from South Africa." Such insinuations were reminiscent of Jimmy Carter's suggestion, that Israel is a "racist, apartheid state." It is important to recall that on March 15, 1975 Jimmy Carter declared:

"The Palestinian people must have a homeland or entity and Israel must withdraw to the 1967 borders with minor adjustment."

Now, in the era of Obama, it has become politically correct to call Israel a "Jewish homeland. » In April 2008 Los Angeles Times published a report about Barak Obama's ties to Rashid Khalidi, "a professor of Arab studies at Columbia" who was barred from lecturing in New York public school for accusing Israel as a "racist, apartheid state." Dick Morris said that many American Jews do not find "Obama's ties to Rashid Khalidi and other radicals alarming because they are not concerned with self-preservation." The "progressive" American Jews feel safe in America. In Leon Feuchtwanger's novel Jew Suess (Sweet Jew) this Jew lived a life of privilege at the court of a

German king, but at the end was hanged for being Jewish. The Israelis struggle for their self-preservation. They are surrounded by enemies who want to destroy them. Former Secretary of State Lawrence Eagleburger stated that the election of Obama poses a threat to the stability of the Middle East. He calls Obama a "charlatan," citing his murky past, his ties to radicals as well as his many "flip-flops." Jimmy Carter, who supported Obama in 2008 and 2012 elections, also used to proclaim his support of Israel, but his presidency had turned out to be Israel's nightmare. After only 2 days in office Obama called for a total freeze of Israeli construction in the West Bank. He also advocated "two state solutions in the peace process in the Arab-Israeli conflict," but in his State of the Union speech in January 2011 Obama did not say a word about the "peace process" and 'two state solution of the Arab-Israeli conflict." This does not mean that he will scale down his pressure on Israel. He would not be able to resist his temptation to press for Israeli concessions which is a part of his ideological DNA. Obama used to say to the voters:

"It is not about me, it is about you!"

It has always been about him and his self-aggrandizement.

Obama will cast aside his supporters as he had cast aside and walk over Rev. Jeremiah Wright, Lois Farrakhan, Rashid Khalidi, William Ayers, Antoun Resko and others whom he no longer needed. Obama's political cunning and verbal virtuosity will at some point made him stumble over some issues like the Obama care. But he will break his political neck by trying to extract Israel's concessions. Obama's scythe will hit Israeli rock. Barack Obama, the Talker-in-Chief, is an eloquent orator who has, as the Russian saying goes, a "boneless tongue." It is enough to hear him wiggle out of the Rev. Jeremiah Wright deadly noose, out of the endorsement by Lois Farrakhan, out of ties to the Rashid Khalidi and the Weather Underground terrorist William Ayers, and so on. He changes his claims and denials as a chameleon changes its colors. He is a gifted political con-artist or, as Lawrence Eagleburger called him, a "charlatan." But there is no evil without some good in it. With Barak Obama in the White House, the world will know that Americans are not racist, mean and intolerant people. America will survive Obama and Israel will survive him too - it survived Carter. After Carter came Reagan. Hopefully, after Obama a Reagan-like president will be elected.

Mike Huckabee visited Israel in mid-August 2009 and expressed **very** different views than what the mainstream American media had been exposing. He stated that Israel should not allow evacuation or limiting of settlements construction of settlements and should not allow a creation of a Palestinian state in the land of Israel and not allow a division of Jerusalem. He said: "If the Palestinians really want a state, they should create their state on the empty land, stretching from the Indian Ocean to the Atlantic in the Arab countries." If the Arab countries really wanted a state for the Palestinians, the Arab countries can give a state to Palestinians, but they and the Palestinians want to destroy the Jewish state and expel all infidel Jews from their midst. Obama's obsession with Israel and his fixation on demanding the settlements freeze reminds me of an old anecdote about a man who was about to be released from a mental institution. He was examined by psychiatrists who asked him what he would do, if they let him go home. He said that he would go to a park, sit on a bench and invite to his home a woman, who was passing by. Then he would kiss and undress her. Up to this point the psychiatrists felt that he was doing fine. But then he said: "You know women have those panties with rubber bands in them. I will take out this rubber band and make a slingshot. Then I would shoot my neighbor." The psychiatrists called their male nurses and asked them to come with a straight jacket.

INTERLUDE: KINDRED SOULS[3]

On November 10 2010 and for the next three days Glen Beck in his program quoted George Soros who in his published books had recalled that during his childhood he had fancied himself to be a "Messiah" and "God" and felt that his mission was to "change the world." Soros revealed that shortly before the German occupation of Hungary, his father had changed their family name from Schwartz to Soros to save his family from the Nazi persecution. Soros also revealed that he as a young boy lived in the German occupied Budapest with the family of a Hungarian official, posing as his godson. This official was the head of the "Jewish Council" which was deporting the Jews to Nazi concentration camps and young Soros was delivering deportation notices to the Jewish families. He later stated that the years of Nazi occupation were "the happiest years of his childhood." He also recalled, "My mother was quite anti-Semitic and ashamed of being Jewish. Given the culture in which we lived, being Jewish was a clear-cut stigma, a disadvantage, a handicap. And therefore, she always had the desire to transcend it, to escape it." Now George Soros gives billions of dollars to all kind of left-wing virulently anti-Israel organizations. He has not contributed a penny to Israel or to the Holocaust survivors. He is a kindred soul of such formerly Jewish Jew-haters as the infamous Inquisitor Tomás de Torquemada and Stalin's henchman Lazar Kaganovich, who in 1942 did not object to Stalin's order to execute Mikhail Kaganovich, Lazar brother. In 1953, on the eve of Stalin's death, the Soviet dictator ordered Lazar Kaganovich to direct the deportation of the Soviet Jews to Siberia.

The British newspaper Daily Telegraph in an article on October 3, 2009 declared *"Mahmud Ahmadinejad's vitriolic attacks on the Jewish world hide reported astonishing secret." The article had* a photo with caption "A

---

[3] This article mentions several known to history anti-Semites

photograph of the Iranian president holding up his identity card during elections in March 2008. This card clearly shows his family has Jewish roots." The article stated: "A close-up of the document reveals he was previously known as Sabourjian. The short note scrawled on the card suggests his family changed its name to Ahmadinejad when they converted to Islam after his birth. The Sabourjians traditionally came from Aradan, Mr. Ahmadinejad's birthplace, and the name derives from word 'Sabour,' the name for the Jewish Tallit shawl in Persia. This name is even on the list of reserved names for Iranian Jews compiled by Iran's Ministry of the Interior. Experts last night suggested that Mr. Ahmadinejad's track record for hate-filled attacks on Jews could be an overcompensation to hide his past."

Hitler dreaded the thought that he had a Jewish ancestor and ordered his lawyer Hans Frank to investigate his lineage. Frank discovered that Hitler's grandmother Maria Anna Schickelgruber had become pregnant while working as a house cleaner in a Jewish household in Graz, Austria. She gave birth to a son, whom she named Alois, leaving the father's name blank on Alois's birth certificate. Hitler's grandmother later married Johann Georg Hitler, who adopted Alois, Adolph Hitler's father. The thought that a Jew had fathered Alois haunted Hitler his whole life.

Similarly, Stalin, a Georgian, was incensed by Niko Marr's theory of the Semitic origin of the Georgian language. Shortly before his death Stalin launched a campaign to disgrace the Academician Marr, who had died some twenty years earlier and could not be arrested. So Stalin ordered arrests of all of Marr's disciples.

Ahmadinejad, Stalin and Hitler were pathological Jew haters. History abounds with leaders who believed that they were "Messiahs." and "Gods." Invariably, these leaders were products of the traumatic experiences in their childhood from which they emerged with an uncanny ability to manipulate and mesmerize people. Their maniacal convictions in their divinity proved to be contagious for many people.

2012: OBAMA, KERRY AND HAGEL

On December 21, 2012 The Jewish Week published an article by Stewart Ain, titled "Hagel at Pentagon Could Spell More U.S. – Israel Tension." The subtitle read: "Kerry at State would not cause concern among most Jewish groups" The article quotes Aaron David Miller stating:

"John Kerry is safe, centrist, loyal and comfortable as secretary of state."

Mainstream media promoted Kerry as "decorated Vietnam War veteran," but did not mention his prominent role in the anti-Vietnam War movement. This "decorated Vietnam War veteran" threw away his medal ribbons in protest against the Vietnam War. Kerry testified before the Senate Foreign Relations Committee, stating:

American soldiers were committing war crimes, not isolated incidents, but crimes committed on a day-to-day basis with the full awareness of officers at all level of command. 200,000 Vietnamese were murdered by the United States of America. » Kerry testified about American "atrocities in Vietnam," accusing American soldiers of "rapes, beheadings, torture and pillaging in a fashion reminiscent of Genghis Khan."

At that time Weather Underground terrorist William Ayers and his comrades were exploding bombs under American institutions. The anti-war hippies gathered in Woodstock, smoking marihuana, denouncing "American war criminals" and shouting: » Make Love, not war." It became fashionable to burn American flags and to dodge the draft. Such political turmoil persisted during the 1972 election in which Nixon was running against George McGovern who was running as the anti-Vietnam War candidate. John McCain at that time was tortured in the North Vietnamese prison. Despite poisonous anti-Nixon propaganda, Nixon won the 1972 election by the greatest landslide in

American history. He lost only one state, Massachusetts, the bluest of the blue states. In October 2004 John Kerry addressed audience at the Arab-American Institute and declared:

"I know how disheartened Palestinians are by the Israeli government's decision to build a barrier, increasing the hardship of the Palestinian people. We do not need another barrier to peace. "Kerry worried that this barrier would "increase the hardship of the Palestinian people" and ignored the fact that the Israeli people were "disheartened" by being blown up to pieces by Palestinian terrorists. To attract the Jewish vote, Kerry emphasized his commitment to Israeli security and said repeatedly that he would ask for the support of the United Nations without mentioning the well-known fact of anti-Israel UN majority. In 2012 Kerry was coaching Obama to spin his boneless tongue, which Obama has been spinning quite well since his days as community organizer in Chicago.

As for Chuck Hagel, it was not the first time that President Obama promoted him. In 2009 he named retired Sen. Chuck Hagel to co-chair the President's Intelligence Advisory Board, although Hagel was considered a harsh critic of Israel by many pro-Israel activists during his two terms in the Senate, which ended early in 2009. Hagel told an Arab-American group in 2007 that his support for Israel was not "automatic," and in an interview with Middle East negotiator Aaron David Miller he said: "The Jewish lobby intimidates a lot of people on Capitol Hill. » Hagel also was one of a handful of senators who didn't sign AIPAC-backed letters related to Israel and during his time in the Senate opposed additional sanctions on Iran. The Jewish Week article quoted Gerald Steinberg, a professor of political science at Bar-Ilan University in Israel, who said: "Hegel has a clear track record of hostility towards Israel… He could slow down the delivery of weapons to Israel, and Israel might act alone against Iran."

Isi Libeler in his December 23, 2012 article in the Jerusalem Post wrote: » The possible nomination of former Republican Senator Chuck Hagel as Secretary of Defense will represent a litmus test as to whether

President Obama is poised to resume his anti-Israeli campaign. Hegel is supported by the wrong people. These include the Council on American Islamic Relation (CAIR), described by FBI as an unindicted co-conspirator to fund Hamas and also cited as an agent of the Muslim Brotherhood in America.

Stephen Walt, co-author of the notorious book 'The Israel Lobby and US Foreign Policy," who mimicked classic anti-Semitic stereotypes, said: "Hegel's nomination could be excellent, because unlike almost all of his former colleagues on the Capital Hill, he is skeptical about the use of military force against Iran. The appointment would represent Obama's payback to Benjamin Netanyahu."

Isi Libeler also wrote: "As far as 1999, Hagel was he only Senator who refused to sign a letter urging Russian President Yeltsin to take action to quash burgeoning anti-Semitism."

The Jewish Week article stated that the nomination of Kerry or Hagel "would not cause concern among most Jewish groups. " In 1980 78% of the Jewish vote went for Jimmy Carter, whose presidency turned out to be Israel's nightmare. 78% of Jews voted for Barack Obama in 2008. In 2012 election this percentage shrunk to 69%, as more American Jews began to feel the Obama drift.

Early in Obama presidency an AP report stated:

In his first foreign policy speech since clinching the Democratic nomination in the U.S. presidential race Barack Obama assured the American Israel Public Affairs Committee (AIPAC) that he would not allow Iran to acquire nuclear arms, and that Jerusalem would remain the undivided capital of Israel. He said: "Let me be clear, Israel's security is sacrosanct. It is non-negotiable. The Palestinians need a state that is contiguous and cohesive and that allows them to prosper. But any agreement with the Palestinian people must preserve Israel's identity as a Jewish state, with secure, recognized and defensible borders. Jerusalem will remain the capital of Israel and it must remain undivided." He said this to secure the Jewish vote. In a move that shocked his AIPAC audience but which his supporters called "brave," Barack Obama dropped his drawers to prove that he was Jewish. John McCain immediately issued a statement, alleging that he was circumcised first. (The Republican candidate is 71.) Basing himself on extensive fieldwork, Daniel Pipes, a McCain supporter and noted authority on Muslim culture, observes: "Looks can be deceiving -- Muslims are also circumcised." (Pipes' new book is "Turkish Bath Terror Network.") Speaking for the Democratic Party, Nancy Pelosi promises to investigate the "particulars" of their candidate. Meanwhile, Hillary Clinton announced that although as a feminist she opposed circumcision, she would make an exception if it would get her the nomination. "Speaking as her husband," Bill Clinton said, "I couldn't care less, but if this is what it takes, heck, I'll slice off a piece too." Crackers from Hope refused comment.

Abraham Katsman in his **25/01/2010** article *"Obama has made his own personality and identity cornerstones of US diplomacy."* wrote:

Obama, more than any recent president, has made his own personality and identity cornerstones of American diplomacy. He assumes his potent charm can bend America's adversaries his way that American history began anew on January 20, 2009 and that hostilities can be resolved through dialogue with him. His tactic of choice has been to visit a troubled region, apologize to the local authoritarians for America's sinful pre-Obama history, disavow acts of previous administrations and suggest that he brings with him a diplomatic "reset-button" Obama's belief in his own powers was reinforced by a love-struck press. After his vaguely messianic campaign and inauguration, Newsweek's Evan Thomas typified the mood, hyperventilating that Obama was "standing above the country... above the world. He's sort of God." But once president, reality intruded: The leaders of Russia, China and North Korea don't believe in God. And the Islamist God is somewhat less warm and fuzzy than Barack Obama.

On May 14, 2010 The Associated Press reported:

Russian President Dmitry Medvedev and US President Barack Obama on Thursday discussed Iran's suspect nuclear program and the need to look for "non-standard" approaches to resolving problems in the Middle East, the Kremlin said. Their telephone conversation, which the Kremlin said lasted for an hour and a half, came as the United States tries to build support for new sanctions against Iran. The Kremlin said Medvedev briefed Obama about his trip this week to Syria and Turkey, where he had made clear Moscow's willingness to play an active part in efforts to bring peace to the Middle East. The United States opposes a joint Turkish-Brazilian effort that could help Iran avoid new United Nations sanctions. Medvedev, who met with Turkey's president on Wednesday in Ankara, plays host to Brazil's president in Moscow on Friday. Obama and Medvedev "according to tradition exchanged opinions at great length on the Iranian nuclear problem," the Kremlin statement said. They agreed to intensify efforts to work out a common position within the framework of the six key powers, the five permanent UN Security Council members plus Germany, it said. The two presidents, who plan to meet in the US in June, also agreed to work together more actively on the situation in the Middle East, "including studying non-standard approaches," the statement said. The United States and its allies accuse Iran of seeking to develop nuclear weapons, and the UN has demanded Teheran halt uranium enrichment, a process that can be used to produce either nuclear fuel or a warhead. Iran says its program is peaceful and that it has a right to pursue enrichment to power reactors to generate electricity. The UN has already imposed three rounds of financial sanctions over its refusal.

On November 28, 2013 Jerusalem Post reported:

US President Barack Obama has asked Prime Minister Binyamin Netanyahu to "take a breather" from his vocal criticism of the interim deal signed in Geneva, journalist David Ignatius wrote in a column published in The Washington Post. Obama and Netanyahu spoke on the phone on Sunday, in a conversation meant to assuage the prime minister's concerns following the signing of the "first stage" deal between Tehran and the P5+1 countries.

US President Obama and Prime Minister Netanyahu on the phone. Photo: REUTERS

Obama said:

Your grandparents had to risk their lives and all that they had to make a place for themselves in this world. Your parents lived through war after war to ensure the survival of the Jewish state. Iran must know this time is not unlimited. And I've made the position of the United States of America clear: Iran must not get a nuclear weapon. As President, I've said all options are on the table for achieving our objectives. America will do what we must to prevent a nuclear-armed Iran.

Obama in Israel, 2013

On November 25, 2013 Associated Press published an article *"Obama has been secretly negotiating with Iran for months"*

WASHINGTON - *The United States and Iran secretly engaged in a series of high-level, face-to-face talks over the past year, in a high-stakes diplomatic gamble by the Obama administration that paved the way for the historic deal sealed early Sunday in Geneva aimed at slowing Tehran's nuclear program. The discussions were kept hidden even from America's closest friends, including its negotiating partners and Israel, until two months ago, and that may explain how the nuclear accord appeared to come together so quickly after years of stalemate and fierce hostility between Iran and the West. The talks were held in the Middle Eastern nation of Oman and elsewhere with only a tight circle of people in the know... Since March, Deputy Secretary of State William Burns and, Vice President Joe Biden's top foreign policy adviser, have met at least five times with Iranian officials. The last four clandestine meetings, held since Iran's reform-minded President Hassan Rouhani was inaugurated in August, produced much of the agreement later formally hammered out in negotiations in Geneva among the United States,*

The U.S. and Iran cut off diplomatic ties in 1979 after the Islamic Revolution and the storming of the U.S. Embassy in Tehran, where 52 Americans were held hostage for more than a year. But Obama has expressed willingness since becoming president to meet with the Iranians without conditions. At the president's direction, the United States began a tentative outreach shortly after his inauguration in January 2009. Obama and Iran's supreme leader, Ayatollah Ali Khamenei, exchanged letters, but the engagement yielded no results. That outreach was hampered by Iran's hardliner former president, Mahmoud Ahmedinejad, whose re-election in a disputed vote in June of that year led to a violent crackdown on opposition protesters.... The secret informal discussions between mid-level officials in Washington and Tehran began. Officials described those early contacts as exploratory discussions focused on the logistics of setting up higher-level talks. The talks took on added weight eight months ago, when Obama dispatched the deputy secretary of state Burns, the top aide Sullivan and five other officials to meet with their Iranian counterparts in the Omani capital of Muscat. Obama dispatched the group shortly after the six powers opened a new round of nuclear talks with Iran in Almaty, Kazakhstan, in late February.

It was only after that Obama-Rouhani phone call that the U.S. began informing allies of the secret talks with Iran, the U.S. officials said. Obama handled the most sensitive conversation himself, briefing Israeli Prime Minister Benjamin Netanyahu during a Sept. 30 meeting at the White House. He informed Netanyahu only about the two summer meetings, not the March talks, in keeping with the White House's promise only to tell allies about any discussions with Iran that were substantive. The U.S. officials would not describe Netanyahu's reaction. But the next day, he delivered his General Assembly speech, blasting Rouhani as a "wolf in sheep's clothing" and warning the U.S. against mistaking a change in Iran's tone with an actual change in nuclear ambitions. The Israeli leader has subsequently denounced the potential nuclear agreement as the "deal of the century" for Iran. After telling Netanyahu about the secret talks, the United States then briefed the other members of the six-nation negotiating team...

When riots threatened Egyptian President Mubarak's regime, Obama did not send a general to urge Mubarak to leave the county. He sent Frank Wisner, "an influential retired diplomat and former US ambassador to Egypt, who met with Mubarak at President Barack Obama's request." The AFP report on February 5, 2011 sent the media talking heads spinning out of control in disbelieve. The report stated:

"Wisner called Mubarak an old friend of the United States, and said he must stay in office in order to steer those changes through. President Mubarak's continued leadership is critical. It's his opportunity to write his own legacy. He has given 60 years of his life to the service of his country, this is an ideal moment for him to show the way forward."

After publication of this report Hillary Clinton stated:

"Wisner was speaking for himself and not for the US government,"

Despite Cairo "pro-democracy" crowds demands for Mubarak to

"resign and for the transition of power to start immediately," Mubarak decided to stay in office. According to the ABC News report on February 3, 2011 Mubarak struck a defiant tone, telling ABC News correspondent Christiana Amanpour that he would "never run away" and would "die on the soil of Egypt." He said that he was ready to leave office, but could not do that for fear his country would sink deeper into chaos. He told her:

"I am fed up. After 62 years in public service, I have had enough. I want to go but I am troubled by the deadly violence between anti- and pro-government groups in Tahrir Square. The government was not responsible for it. I blame the outlawed Muslim Brotherhood for the violence. I do not intend to have my son Gamal assume the presidency. I had a phone conversation with US President Barack Obama earlier this week and I told him, 'You don't understand the Egyptian culture. What would happen if I step down now? Looting and arson would erupt."

In societies, which never before knew democracy, the will of the majority may lead to a tyranny in which brutality and denial of human rights far exceed what prevailed in the previous autocratic or dictatorial regimes. This happened with the Bolshevik tyranny in Russia, which proved far worse than the tsarist autocracy, and with the nightmarish regime of the ayatollahs which replaced the autocratic rule of the Shah. The slogans "freedom and democracy" were popular in January 1979 in Iran just before the Shah was forced to leave Iran and that country was taken over by Khomeini fanatics.

The blaming America for its support of "corrupt regimes" in Iran and in Vietnam was at the root of the tragedies that happened in these countries. The choice in Iran was between the Shah's imperfect pro-Western government and the bestiality of the Islamic fanatics led by

Ayatollah Khomeini, while the choice in South Vietnam was between the bestiality of the communist dictatorship in North Vietnam and the imperfect democracy of the South. The war of terror against the United States began with Ayatollah Khomeini's call for "Death to America!" The Iranian Jews were the first victims of the Ayatollah's lunacy. The ancient Jewish community that had survived in Persia for two-and-one-half millennia was no more. The synagogue in the city of Shiraz, the traditional place of the Tomb of Queen Esther, was left with no Jews to glorify her for saving the Jewish people from their enemy Haman. The few remaining Jews of Shiraz were imprisoned as "Israeli spies." As the Iranian Jews were being driven out of Iran, the Jewish emigration from the Soviet Union came to an abrupt halt on December 25, 1979, the day the Soviets invaded Afghanistan. The Soviets were emboldened by Carter's hostility toward Israel and his policy that led to the Khomeini takeover in Iran. The Soviet leaders intended to occupy Afghanistan to encircle China when clashes along the 2000 miles long Soviet-Chinese border intensified. The Soviets had pursued the same goal of encircling China by supporting North Vietnam. This is why President Nixon wanted to strike an implicit alliance with China by sending Henry Kissinger and then went to China himself to shake Mao's hand.

Mohammed ElBaradei, former Chairman of International Atomic Energy Agency, returned to Egypt, demanding "immediate resignation" of Mubarak while ElBaradei was presented by the media as the "voice of Egyptian people." The Muslim Brotherhoods rode to power on the back of ElBaradei, using him as its Trojan Horse and demanded creation of an "anti-Mubarak coalition of opposition group, headed by ElBaradei." On December 10, 2005 ElBaradei was awarded the Nobel Peace Prize, thus joining Yasser Arafat and Jimmy Carter as a beneficiary of the Nobel Prize Committee's some of the most memorable and shameful gaffes. After he received the Nobel Peace Prize award ElBaradei stated:

"No smoking gun had emerged to prove Iran's intent was horrible."

Where ElBaradei does not see a smoking gun, Israelis see a mushroom cloud. ElBaradei believed that "stripping" Israel of its very existence might be the key to achieving peace in the Middle East. Luckily, the Muslim Brotherhood was in power in Egypt only briefly and was replaced Mubarak by Egyptian army rebellion.

On January 20, 2013 Obama began his second presidential term and on January 22, 2013 Israelis voted in the Knesset election and Netanyahu began forming Israel's new government. A new period of tension began in the relations between Obama and Netanyahu. Iran will soon cross the red line which Netanyahu mentioned in his UN speech. After his re-election in 2012 Obama visited Israel and started his rhetorical charm offensive. He spoke to young Israeli students about the suffering of the Palestinian people. He also tried to convince Netanyahu and the Israeli people that Iranian leaders will eventually agree to terminate their nuclear program. I believe that Obama's preaching will not deter Israeli leaders from defending their country from the Iranian nuclear threat.

Bryan Fischer, in his article *"Clueless or complicit: Obama and Islam's war with on America"* published on August 12, 2014 in "Focal Point with Bryant Fischer, stated: *"President Obama is not our commander-in-chief, but Islam's enabler-in-chief."*

OBAMA'S NARCISSISM

I am not a psychologist, but I pay attention to the opinions to people who are. After visiting several countries in the Far East, Obama said:

"I am the first Pacific President."

The next day Charles Krauthammer, a licensed psychiatrist, who modestly calls himself a "psychiatrist in remission," said on Fox News:

"Obama is afflicted by a colossal narcissism."

In 2008 I read Dr. Sam Vaknin's book *Malignant Self Love* and several of his articles on narcissism. I thought that Dr. Vaknin might be interested in reading my Carter book and sent it to him. In his e-mail to me Dr. Vaknin wrote:

"I just finished reading your book about Carter. It is as compelling as it was thrilling. Now that Carter has assumed the mantle of "Defender of the Palestinians" it may be time to re-issue it and remind everyone who this man really is. I wish it were in me to write an equally thorough study of Obama. There are so many similarities between these two Democratic Presidents, it is positively unnerving! I want to express my greatest appreciation and my heartfelt gratitude for sharing this with me. I posted information about your book to my various mailing lists."

In my reply to Dr. Vaknin I wrote:

"I also find many similarities between Carter and Obama. The difference is that Obama is by far a much more eloquent demagogue then Carter, and this makes him much more dangerous"

Following Dr. Vaknin's advice, I re-published my Carter book in November 2010.

On August 11, 2008 Dr. Vaknin published his article *"Barack Obama -*

Narcissist or Merely Narcissistic?" in which he stated:

"Granted, only a qualified mental health diagnostician (which I am not) can determine whether someone suffers from Narcissistic Personality Disorder (NPD) and this, following lengthy tests and personal interviews. But, in the absence of access to Barack Obama, one has to rely on his overt performance and on testimonies by his closest advisers. Narcissistic leaders are... subtle, refined, socially-adept, manipulative, possessed of thespian skills, and convincing... Perhaps it is time to require each candidate to high office in the USA to submit to a rigorous physical and mental checkup with the results made public. Obama's early life was decidedly chaotic and replete with traumatic and mentally bruising dislocations. Mixed-race marriages were even less common then. His parents went through a divorce when he was an infant (two years old). Obama saw his father only once again, before he died in a car accident. Then, his mother re-married and Obama had to relocate to Indonesia: a foreign land with a radically different culture, to be raised by a step-father. At the age of ten, he was whisked off to live with his maternal (white) grandparents. He saw his mother only intermittently in the following few years and then she vanished from his life in 1979. She died of cancer in 1995. Pathological narcissism is a reaction to prolonged abuse and trauma in early childhood or early adolescence. The source of the abuse or trauma is immaterial: the perpetrators could be dysfunctional or absent parents, teachers, other adults, or peers. The narcissist feels grandiose and self-important (e.g., exaggerates accomplishments, talents, skills, contacts, and personality traits to the point of lying, demands to be recognized as superior without commensurate achievements); Is obsessed with fantasies of unlimited success, fame, fearsome power or omnipotence, unequalled brilliance... convinced that he or she is unique and, being special... Requires excessive admiration, adulation... Behaves arrogantly and haughtily... Feels superior, omnipotent, omniscient, invincible....Rages when frustrated, contradicted, or confronted by people he or she considers inferior to him or her and unworthy. Perhaps the most immediately evident trait of patients with Narcissistic Personality Disorder (NPD) is their vulnerability to criticism and disagreement. Subject to negative input, real or imagined, even to a mild rebuke, a constructive suggestion, or an offer to help, they feel injured, humiliated and empty and they react with disdain (devaluation), rage, and defiance."

Dr. Vaknin suggests that narcissists are driven by a hidden desire to avenge their childhood traumas and they develop personality traits, which explain why they succeed in mesmerizing masses of people. Several commentators mention narcissism as explanation for Obama polices, among them George Will, who stated on the Fox News Special Report program:

"Obama is afflicted by narcissistic policy disorder."

A New York Post reader John W. McGinley in *New York Post Letters, February 15, 2010* wrote:

"Rich Lowry has it right - President Obama just doesn't get it. But Obama is also burdened with a severe narcissistic disorder, and our country is paying the price. He is addicted to hearing what he considers to be his oh-so-nuanced public pronouncements"

It is really not important whether Obama was born in Hawaii or in Kenya. It was also not important that Lenin was born in Simbirsk, a small provincial town in Russia, or that Stalin was born in Gori, a small town in Georgia, or that Hitler was born in Braun am Inn, a small town in Austria, or that Napoleon was born in Ajaccio, a town in Corsica. But it is important to understand the psychological peculiarities of these rulers that explain their ability to inspire adoration from millions of people. These Vozhds (Russian for Rulers), Fuhrers and Emperors ruled in countries which had with traditions of absolute monarchies for centuries. The question is: Why was Barack Obama able to be twice elected president of the United States, a country with strong democratic traditions, free press and open access to information?

In my Carter book I quoted Senator John Tower who said that Jimmy Carter had "Messiah complex." I also quoted several passages from Ernest Jones' two volume book "Psycho-Myth, Psycho-History." He wrote:

"We find even minor prophets and preachers speaking in the name of God with the authorities so astonishing as to preclude the idea of its arising solely in learning; in other words, one feels sure that their conscious attitude is generally the product of an unconscious fantasy in which they identify their personality with that of God.... Such a megalomaniac fantasy would be barely comprehensible did we not know how closely the idea of God and father are associated, so that from a purely psychological point of view they may be regarded as magnified, idealized, and projected form of the idea of Father.... There emerges a princely, stern, and sometime caring father figure, who is feared but whose protection is longed for – Freud's Great Man.... "Freud's Great Man display tendency to aloofness, omniscience, omnipotence, which are manifestations of colossal narcissism...." The unresolved inner conflict of great men generates an inherently ambivalent, but immensely powerful force, which when either exaggerated or not properly directed by firm moral standards and misguided by false sense of values could be enormously destructive."

Sigmund Freud wrote:

Why the great man should rise to significance at all we have no doubt whatsoever. We know that the great majority of people have a strong need for authority which they can admire, to which they can submit, and which dominates and sometimes even ill-treats them. The great man influences his contemporaries in one of two ways- through his personality and through the ideas for which he stands. Sometimes – and this is surely the more primitive effect – the personality alone exerts its influence, and the idea plays a decidedly subordinate role.

In my Carter book I wrote:

"By identifying his own traumas with those of the nation, Carter was projecting on the nation and the world his inner unresolved conflicts. This type of projection could not but lead to a perpetuation and magnification of national and world strife. Carter has a very effective method to mesmerize and compel people to read into him and his demagoguery anything they desire or hope for, turning them into dupes and

accomplices of his provocations. This method makes it possible for him to escape responsibility and to blame others for the disasters which punctuate his record. ... The problem seems to arise from the conviction of great men that they can solve mankind's problems, and therefore have the moral right to impose, ruthlessly and self-righteously, their will on ordinary people, who are supposedly blind to their own interests. The tragedy is that great men invariably mistake their own salvation for that of mankind."

Carter praised his ability to make "instant analyses" of people:

"Very early I was able - six or seven years old — to judge very accurately who the good people were on the streets of Plains and who the bad people were. The good people were the ones that bought boiled peanuts. The bad ones didn't.

Like Carter, Obama has a very high opinion of his ability to find people who are compatible with him. After being elected, Carter and Obama began selling different kinds of "boiled peanuts" to people in this country. Jimmy Carter often said that he was "born again." In the chapter "Born Again" of my Carter book I quote Carter, who had described how his "born again" miracle happened:

"Some day in May 1967, I and another person, Mio Pennington from Texas, agreed to speak about their faith to some hundred families of non-believers in Lock Haven, Pennsylvania, and to seek their conversion. Milo Pennington, who happens to be a peanut farmer, and who was not well-educated, did the most work and talking. Pennington was then about 70 years old. It seemed to me he was the most inept person I had ever known in expressing himself. He fumbled and didn't know what to say and I thought, 'Oh, I could do much better.... Yet what happened was a miracle: Milo Pennington succeeded in converting fifteen to twenty families during a single week! The whole week was almost a miracle to me and I felt the sense of presence of God's influence in my life."

Milo Pennington recalled:

"From then on, Jimmy Carter acted all the time like he was on the mountaintop for the Lord."

When that miraculous week ended, he called his wife Rosalynn on the phone. She said:

"Jimmy, you don't sound like the same person. You sound like you are intoxicated."

Jimmy agreed:

"Well, in a way I am."

Carter was intoxicated with "a new sense of release and assurance and peace. He wrote:

"When I have a sense of peace and self-assurance that what I am doing is the right thing, I assume, maybe in an unwarranted way, that's doing God's will."

Ernest Jones wrote:

"Such fantasies are not at all rare, and possibly occur here and there all people. There is, however, a class of man with whom it is much stronger than usual, so that it forms a constant and integral part of their unconscious. Such an unusually strong identification with God does not of itself amount to insanity. In a state of sanity, that is to say when the feeling for reality and the normal inhibitions of consciousness are operative, the fantasy can express itself only after passage through this censorship, and therefore only in a modified, weakened, and indirect form."

Eric H. Eriksson in his pioneering work *"Young Man Luther"* pointed out that "a deep nostalgia for an infantile trust, as well as lasting violent doubts about a dangerous father, are underlying factors in a "conversion" experience which stands on the borderline of the psychological and the theological."

Barack Obama did not say that he was born again. I suspect that he acquired a "sense of peace and self-assurance" during his work as a "community organizer," when people in his community responded with applauds and adoration to his rhetoric.

In my Stalin book I wrote about the childhood traumas of Stalin, Hitler and Lenin. Dorothy Carrington in her book *"Napoleon and His Family"* quoted Napoleon's letter, which he had written to his relatives when he was 20 years old:

I was born when the nation was perishing. Thirty thousand Frenchmen spewed on the coasts, engulfing the throne of liberty in seas of blood: such was the odious sight that first met my eyes. The cries of the dying, the groans of the oppressed, and tears of despair surrounded my cradle from the hour of my birth.

2014: GAZA WAR – MAN VS PUNK

During the summer of 2014 the Israel-Hamas war erupted. On July 26, 2014 DEBKA file reported:

After Hamas fired hundreds of rockets into Israel in the summer of 2014, the Israeli Army attacked network of tunnels which Hamas had built in Gaza for infiltration of terrorists into Israel. Israel's security and policy cabinet in Jerusalem and Hamas leaders in the Gaza Strip and Qatar Friday, July 25, 2014 decided to reject the "humanitarian" seven-day ceasefire put before them by US Secretary of State John Kerry.

On August 1, 2014 DEBKA file reported:

Prime Minister Binyamin Netanyahu was wavering Sunday, July 27, between sticking with his pact with Saudi Arabia and Egypt to crush Hamas - at the cost of a deep rift with Washington - or going along with Kerry, at the cost of Israel's security against dangerous terrorists. This dilemma was mirrored in the stop-go ceasefire orders to Israel's forces fighting in the Gaza Strip. Halfway measures will not go down well with the Israeli public, which, even after losing 43 servicemen in action in the Gaza Strip, is still solidly behind the operation. A poll conducted by TV Channel 10 found 87 percent of those canvassed demanding that Israel press on, and 69 percent urging the government to go all the way and overthrow Hamas. Prime Minister Binyamin Netanyahu, Defense Minister Moshe Ya'alon and Chief of Staff Lt. Gen. Benny Gantz made a joint TV appearance Monday with a pledge to continue the campaign against Hamas until all its goals were achieved, Netanyahu, Ya'alon, Gantz pledge to carry on war on Hamas Gen. Gantz said: As a human being, it is hard for me to accept civilian deaths - unlike Hamas, which is solely responsible for launching from its grounds a missile aimed at Tel Aviv which exploded prematurely. President Barack Obama told Prime Minister Binyamin Netanyahu that he wants an "immediate, unconditional humanitarian" cease-fire in the war with Gaza as "a strategic imperative." In a phone call Sunday,

Obama referred to the cease-fire proposed by Secretary of State John Kerry which was rejected unanimously on Friday by Israel's security Cabinet. Israel believes Kerry's proposal would lead to rewarding an illegitimate group. An official in Cairo reported that Egyptian army kills 14 al Qaeda terrorists, arrests 47 in Sinai in Egyptian army raids in northern Sinai Friday. The force also destroyed 36 houses and 40 shelters used by jihadist groups as well as 5 cars and 12 motorcycles. Palestinian bomb car intercepted on its way to Jerusalem: A car loaded with gas canisters linked to a large explosive charge was stopped Sunday on its way to Jerusalem at the Beitar Ilit checkpoint southeast of the capital and its Palestinian driver taken into custody. He first tried to escape and kept on driving - even after a Border Police officer tried to jump onto the passenger seat to switch of the engine. He only pulled up and surrendered when the officer pulled a gun at him.

On Aug 1, 2014 Barack Obama told Prime Minister Binyamin Netanyahu that he wants an *"immediate, unconditional humanitarian cease-fire in the war with Gaza as a strategic imperative."* Also on August 1, 2014 John Kerry said that the U.S. condemned the *"outrageous violation of the cease-fire"* and called on Hamas to *"immediately and unconditionally release the missing Israeli soldier."*

Obama's and Kerry's "immediate and unconditional" orders were ignored by Israel and Hamas.

On Oct 17, 2014 *IPA* News reported:

Israeli government officials are fuming over statement made by Secretary of State John Kerry at a State Department reception celebrating the Muslim Eid al-Adha holiday, in which he connected the ongoing Israeli-Palestinian conflict to waves of international recruits flocking to the terrorist group ISIS (which seeks to establish an Islamic caliphate in Syria, Iraq and beyond) to Israeli-Palestinian conflict, saying it "gives a boost to global terrorism".

Kerry said:

"As I went around and met with people in the course of our discussions about the ISIL coalition, the truth is – there wasn't a leader I met with in the region who didn't raise with me spontaneously the need to try to get peace between Israel and the Palestinians, because it was a cause of recruitment and of street anger and agitation that they felt – and I see a lot of heads nodding – they had to respond to."

Naftali Bennett, the Israeli economy minister, blasted Kerry for linking ISIS to Israeli-Palestinian conflict, stating:

John Kerry gives a boost to global terrorism by implying that the beheading earlier this month of British aid worker Alan Henning was caused by the Israeli-Palestinian conflict. It turns out that even when a British Muslim beheads a British Christian, there will always be those who blame the Jews.

The killer, believed to be the same man who beheaded American journalists James Foley and Steven Satloff, spoke with a British accent

Something new is happening in the Middle East. Alliances are shifting. Obama negotiates with Turkey and Qatar, which are mortal enemies of Israel, while Turkey and Qatar are allied with Hamas. Israel is supported by Egypt, Saudi Arabia, Kuwait, and Arab Emirates and by growing number of other Arab states. Benny Avni in his article *"Where's Waldo?"* which *was* published in New York Post on November 7, 2013, quoted Ali al-Ahmed, president of the Washington-based Institute for Gulf Affairs, who said: *"The Saudis don't care about the Palestinians, they care about Iran."* Seth Lipsky In his article *"Gray Lady's 'Israel Lobby' Fixation,"* which was published in New York Post on November 21, 2013, wrote that New York Times correspondent Thomas Friedman in his cable headlined *"Let's Make a Deal,"* which was sent from the United Arab Emirates, complained: *"Never have I seen Israel and America's core Arab allies working more in concert to stymie a major foreign policy initiative of a sitting U.S. president and never have I seen more lawmakers - Democrats and Republicans - more willing to take Israel's side against their own president*

"

Photos of Obama and Netanyahu in their early 20's. Photo of Netanyahu shows him in his days with the Israeli elite Sayeret Matkal commando unit. Photo of; Obama shows him in his dope smoking days as community organizer.

There were many responses to these two photos. One of them was: *"Man vs. Punk"*

In his eloquent and powerful speech at the United Nations General Assembly at U.N. headquarters Benjamin Netanyahu said:

"To defeat ISIS and leave Iran as a potential nuclear power is to win the battle and lose the war. Don't be fooled by Iran's manipulative charm offensive. It's designed for one purpose and for one purpose only: to lift the sanctions and remove the obstacles to Iran's path to the bomb."

Netanyahu closed his speech with words of hope for peace with the Palestinians. He mentioned the growing cooperation of some Arab counties with Israel and suggested that support from leaders of all Middle Eastern countries could help in those efforts, stating:

Together, we must recognize the global threat of militant Islam, the primacy of dismantling Iran's nuclear weapons capability, and the indispensable role of Arab states in advancing peace with the Palestinians."

Sept. 29, 2014 - Benjamin Netanyahu, Prime Minister of Israel, speaks during the 69th session of the United Nations General Assembly at U.N. headquarters

Caroline Glick, a prominent Israeli journalist and author, on July 29, 2014 published in Jerusalem Post her very perceptive an article "Israel, Hamas and Obama's foreign policy." Below is her article:

When US President Barack Obama phoned Prime Minister Binyamin Netanyahu on Sunday night, in the middle of a security cabinet meeting, he ended any remaining doubt regarding his policy toward Israel and Hamas. Obama called Netanyahu while the premier was conferring with his senior ministers about how to proceed in Gaza. Some ministers counseled that Israel should continue to limit our forces to specific pinpoint operations aimed at destroying the tunnels of death that Hamas has dug throughout Gaza and into Israeli territory. Others argued that the only way to truly destroy the tunnels, and keep them destroyed, is for Israel to retake control over the Gaza Strip. No ministers were recommending that Israel end its operations in Gaza completely. The IDF's discovery of Hamas's Rosh Ha Shana plot was the last straw for any Israeli leftists still harboring fantasies about picking up our marbles and going home. Hamas's plan to use its tunnels to send hundreds of terrorists into multiple Israeli border communities simultaneously and carry out a massacre of unprecedented scope, replete with the abduction of hostages to Gaza, was the rude awakening the Left had avoided since it pushed for Israel's 2005 withdrawal from Gaza.... But then the telephone rang. And Obama told Netanyahu he wants an unconditional "humanitarian" cease-fire that will lead to a permanent one. And he wants it now. And by the way, the eventual terms of that cease-fire must include opening Hamas-controlled Gaza's borders with Egypt and Israel and ending Israel's maritime blockade of the Gaza coast. That is, the cease-fire must allow Hamas to rebuild its arsenal of death and destruction quickly, with US political and financial support.

Until Obama made the call, there was lingering doubt among some

Israelis regarding his intentions. Some thought that US Secretary of State John Kerry might have been acting of his own accord last Friday night when he tried to force Israel to accept Hamas's cease-fire terms. But then Obama made his phone call. And all doubts were dispelled. Kerry is just a loyal steward of Obama's foreign policy. Obama is siding with Hamas, and its Muslim Brotherhood patrons in Qatar and Turkey against Israel and its Sunni Arab supporters – Egypt, Saudi Arabia, Jordan and the United Arab Emirates. The fact that the US's current preference for genocidal, Jew-hating jihadists over the only liberal, pro-American, stable US ally in the Middle East is a White House position…..Consequently, the harshest criticisms of the administration's pro-Hamas position were heard from quarters where rarely a peep of criticism for Obama has been heard. The Israeli Left went ballistic. The Israeli Left has been Obama's ace in the hole since he first ran for office, fresh from the pews in Jeremiah Wright's anti-Semitic church. As rattled as Israelis are over Obama's decision to support Hamas against Israel, Netanyahu made clear in his remarks Monday night that Israel has no choice but to keep fighting until we defeat this barbaric enemy. Netanyahu didn't mention Obama, but it was obvious that he was respectfully refusing to hand Israel's head on a platter to Hamas's friend in the White House….. For the past five years, Americans from all quarters have concluded that the manifold failures of Obama's Middle East policies – from Iraq to Iran, Libya, Afghanistan, Egypt, Syria, Israel, the Palestinian Authority and beyond – owe to a combination of Obama's personal disinterest in foreign affairs and his presumed preference for withdrawal and isolationism over engagement. Obama himself has often encouraged this perception with his endless golf games and his talk about fighting "the war at home." Obama's open, public engagement in Hamas's war against Israel shows that the popular assessment is wrong. Obama is as involved in the Middle East as all of his immediate predecessors were. He is personally leading US policy on every front. Kerry is not an independent actor. The problem is that in every war, in every conflict and in every contest of wills that has occurred in the Middle

East since Obama took office, he has sided with Iran and the Muslim Brotherhood, against America's allies. Under Obama, America has switched sides.

Peter Wehner in his article "Obama's Irrational Animus for Israel" published in Commentary Magazine on August 28, 2014 wrote:

According to the Jerusalem Post, *Martin Indyk, former US special envoy for Israeli-Palestinian Negotiations, wrote: At times US President Barack Obama has become "enraged" at the Israeli government, both for its actions and for its treatment of his chief diplomat, US Secretary of State John Kerry… Gaza has had very negative impact on US-Israel relations The personal relationship between the president and the prime minister has been fraught for some time and it's become more complicated by recent events…. Think about this for a moment. In a neighborhood featuring Hamas, ISIS, Hezbollah, Syria, and Iran, just to name a few of the actors, President Obama was "enraged" at … Israel. That's right, Israel–our stalwart ally, a lighthouse of liberty, lawfulness, and human rights in a region characterized by despotism, and a nation filled with people who long for peace and have done so much for so long to sacrifice for it (including repeatedly returning and offering to return its land in exchange for peace). Yet Mr. Obama–a man renowned for his lack of strong feelings, his emotional equanimity, his disengagement and distance from events, who New York Times columnist Maureen Dowd* refers to *as "Spock" for his Vulcan-like detachment–is not just upset but "enraged" at Israel. Add to this the fact that the conflict with Hamas in Gaza–a conflict started and escalated by Hamas, and in which Hamas used innocent Palestinians as human shields–had a very negative impact on America's relationship with Israel. To show you just how absurd this has become, other Arab nations were siding with Israel in its conflict with Hamas. But not America under Obama. He was constantly applying pressure on Israel. Apparently if you're a nation defending yourself and, in doing so, you wage a war with exquisite care in order to prevent civilian death, it is reason to earn the fury of Mr. Obama. It's clear to me, and by now it should be to others, that there is something sinister in Barack Obama's constant anger aimed at Israel. No previous American president has carried in his heart this degree of hostility for Israel. We can only hope that no future president ever does again. It is a shameful thing to watch this ugliness and irrationality play itself out.*

Bret Stephens in his article *"Obama's Curious Rage,"* which was published in *The Wall Street Journal* on September 2, 2014, also quoted Martin Indyk, who said that Obama is "enraged" when he talks about Israel:

Barack Obama "has become 'enraged' at the Israeli government, both for its actions and for its treatment of his chief diplomat, U.S. Secretary of State John Kerry." So reports the Jerusalem Post, based on the testimony of Martin Indyk, until recently a special Middle East envoy for the president. The war in Gaza, Mr. Indyk adds, has had "a very negative impact" on Jerusalem's relations with Washington. Think about this. Enraged. Not "alarmed" or "concerned" or "irritated" or even "angered." Anger is a feeling. Rage is frenzy. Anger passes. Rage feeds on itself. Anger is specific. Rage is obsession, neurotic. And Mr. Obama — No Drama Obama, the president who prides himself on his cool, a man whose emotional detachment is said to explain his intellectual strength - is enraged. With Israel. Which has just been hit by several thousand unguided rockets and 30-odd terror tunnels, a 50-day war, the forced closure of its one major airport, accusations of "genocide" by Palestinian President Mahmud Abbas, anti-Semitic protests throughout Europe, general condemnation across the world. This is the country that is the object of the president's rage. Ha'arez and the New Republic - both are left-leaning newspapers, which are supporting Obama, but even they cannot understand why the President is enraged by Israel. What kind of person is he? Think about this some more. In the summer in which Mr. Obama became "enraged" with Israel, Islamic State terrorists seized Mosul and massacred Shiite soldiers in open pits, Russian separatists shot down a civilian jetliner, Hamas executed 18 "collaborators" in broad daylight,

Bashar Assad's forces in Syria came close to encircling Aleppo with the aim of starving the city into submission, a brave American journalist had his throat slit on YouTube by a British jihadist, Russian troops openly invaded Ukraine, and Chinese jets harassed U.S. surveillance planes over international waters. Mr. Obama or his administration responded to these events with varying degrees of concern, censure and indignation. But rage?

It is likely that Obama's rage towards Israel is traceable to the time, when he said: *"Some of my most ardent supporters came from the Jewish community in Chicago."* These "ardent supporters" in Chicago convincing him that he has all the Jews in his pocket. Obama later discovered that not all of American Jews succumb to his charm offensive and that most of Israeli Jews do not trust him. Israeli Prime Minister Benjamin Netanyahu rejected Obama's demands and probably this rebuff enraged Obama. Dr. Sam Vaknin wrote:

Perhaps the most immediately evident trait of patients with Narcissistic Personality Disorder (NPD) is their vulnerability to criticism and disagreement. Subject to negative input, real or imagined, even to a mild rebuke, a constructive suggestion, or an offer to help, they feel injured, humiliated and empty and they react with disdain (devaluation), rage, and defiance."

Another explanation for Obama's hostility towards Israel was suggested in the article "Netanyahu's brother-in-law: Obama is an anti-Semite," which was published in the left-leaning Israeli newspaper Ha'arez in March 17, 2012:

Prime Minister Benjamin Netanyahu's brother-in-law Dr. Hagai Ben-Artzi on Wednesday called U.S. President Barack Obama an anti-Semite in an interview with Army Radio. "It's not that Obama doesn't like Bibi," he was referring to Netanyahu, using his nickname). "He doesn't like the nation of Israel." Netanyahu was quick to distance himself from Ben-Artzi's remarks, saying that he completely disagrees with his brother-in-law. Netanyahu said he has a deep appreciation for President Obama's commitment to Israel's security, which he has expressed many times, and also for the deep ties between the two countries. Ben-Artzi was interviewed on Army Radio to provide background on the prime minister. He said: "Look how symbolic it is that your son took part in and won a Bible quiz, whose theme this year is Jerusalem and its connection to Israel, and you, his father, are being tested and asked to prove the strength of the nation of Israel's ties to Jerusalem." Ben-Artzi went on to say that Obama's anti-Semitism stems from years of indoctrination by controversial preacher Rev. Jeremiah Wright, whom Obama distanced himself from during the election campaign. Then Ben-Artzi said: "When there is an anti-Semitic president in the United States, it is a test for us and we have to say: "We will not concede. We are a nation dating back 4,000 years, and you in a year or two will be long forgotten. Who will remember you? But Jerusalem will dwell on forever." Ben-Artzi added that Netanyahu is aware of his views, but declined to say what the two discuss in private conversations.

2014: HURLING INSULTS FROM THE WHITE HOUSE

Jeffrey Goldberg, in his article *"Obama: Israel does not know where its best interests are,"* published on January14, 2013 by *Bloomberg News,* wrote:

"Obama believes that the policy of Netanyahu leads Israel to self-destruction and that Netanyahu leads his country on the road to almost complete isolation. Obama is saying this often and to many people."

In his other article *"The Crisis in U.S.-Israel Relations is officially Here"* published in the Atlantic on October 28, 2014, Jeffrey Goldberg, gleefully described his encounter with two senior White House officials, who knew Goldberg as an ardent Obama supporter, and shared with him what their Commander–in-Chief was telling them about Netanyahu. He wrote:

The other day I was talking to a senior Obama administration official about the foreign leader who seems to frustrate the White House and the State Department the most. "The thing about Bibi is, he's a chickenshit," this official said, referring to the Israeli prime minister, Benjamin Netanyahu, by his nickname. This comment is representative of the gloves-off manner in which American and Israeli officials now talk about each other behind closed doors, and are yet another sign that relations between the Obama and Netanyahu governments have moved toward a full-blown crisis. The relationship between these two administrations - dual guarantors of the putatively "unbreakable" bond between the U.S. and Israel – is now the worst it's ever been, and it stands to get significantly worse after the November midterm elections. By next year, the Obama administration may actually withdraw diplomatic cover for Israel at the United Nations, but even before that, both sides are expecting a showdown over Iran, should an agreement be reached about the future of its nuclear program. Obama administration officials express, in the words of one official, a "red-hot anger" at Netanyahu for pursuing settlement policies on the West Bank, and building policies in Jerusalem, that they believe have fatally undermined Secretary of State John Kerry's peace process. Obama said: 'The Window Is Closing' for a Viable Israel-Palestine Peace Deal" Over the years, Obama administration officials have described Netanyahu to me as recalcitrant, myopic, reactionary, obtuse, blustering, pompous, and "Asperser." (These are verbatim descriptions; I keep a running list.) But I had not previously heard Netanyahu described as a "chickenshit." I thought I appreciated the implication of this description, but it turns out I didn't have a full understanding. From time to time, current and former administration officials have described Netanyahu as a national leader who acts as though he is mayor of Jerusalem, which is to say, a no-vision small-timer who worries mainly about pleasing the hardest core of his political constituency. (President Obama, in interviews with me, has alluded to Netanyahu's lack of political courage.) "The good thing about Netanyahu is that he's scared to launch wars," the official said, expanding the definition of what a chickenshit Israeli prime minister looks like. "The bad thing about him is that he won't do anything to reach an accommodation with the Palestinians or with the Sunni Arab states. The only thing he's interested in is protecting him from political defeat. He's not (Yitzhak) Rabin, he's not (Ariel) Sharon, and he's certainly no (Menachem) Begin. He's got no guts."

I ran this notion by another senior official who deals with the Israel file regularly. This official agreed that Netanyahu is a "chickenshit" on matters related to the comatose peace process, but added that he's also a "coward" on the issue of Iran's nuclear threat. The official said the Obama administration no longer believes that Netanyahu would launch a preemptive strike on Iran's nuclear facilities in order to keep the regime in Tehran from building an atomic arsenal. "It's too late for him to do anything. Two, three years ago, this was a possibility. But ultimately he couldn't bring himself to pull the trigger. It was a combination of our pressure and his unwillingness to do anything dramatic. Now it's too late." U.S. officials had described Netanyahu to me as recalcitrant and pompous." But this was the first time I'd heard him called "chickenshit." This assessment represents a momentous shift in the way the Obama administration sees Netanyahu. In 2010, and again in 2012, administration officials were convinced that Netanyahu and his then-defense minister, the cow boyish ex-commando Ehud Barak, were readying a strike on Iran. To be sure, the Obama administration used the threat of an Israeli strike in a calculated way to convince its allies (and some of its adversaries) to line up behind what turned out to be an effective sanctions regime. But the fear inside the White House of a preemptive attack (or preventative attack, to put it more accurately) was real and palpable—as was the fear of dissenters inside Netanyahu's Cabinet, and at Israel Defense Forces headquarters. At U.S. Central Command headquarters in Tampa, analysts kept careful track of weather patterns and of the waxing and waning moon over Iran, trying to predict the exact night of the coming Israeli attack. Today, there are few such fears. "The feeling now is that Bibi's bluffing," this second official said. "He's not Begin at Osirak," the official added, referring to the successful 1981 Israeli Air Force raid ordered by the ex-prime minister on Iraq's nuclear reactor. The belief that Netanyahu's threat to strike is now an empty one has given U.S. officials room to breathe in their ongoing negotiations with Iran.

In response to Jeffrey Goldberg's October 28 article in The Atlantic, Netanyahu on October 29 in his remarks to the Knesset said:

"I am being attacked because I am willing to defend the State of Israel"

The same day, October 29, Economic Minister Naftali Bennett said:

"Severe curse words against the Israeli Prime Minister are harmful to millions Israeli citizens and Jews worldwide."

Dan Gillerman, Former Israeli Ambassador to the United Nations, said: *"Such name calling is shameful, abusive and counter-productive."*

ROMAN BRACKMAN

ABOUT THE AUTHOR

Roman Brackman was born in Moscow, Russia, in 1931. In 1935 his father, an engineer, was imprisoned in Gulag camp near Dmitrov. As a boy Roman stayed for weeks with his father in the camp's barracks and saw the barb wire, watch towers and columns of prisoners going to and from work. He grew up during the Great Purges when many of his relatives were arrested and perished. He graduated from high school in 1948 and enrolled in the Moscow Oriental Institute, Arabic division, where for two school years he set next to Evgeny Primakov, one of the future Russian Prime Ministers and Foreign Ministers. In 1949 Roman and two of his school friends tried to escape from the Soviet Union by swimming from the Black Sea port Batumi to Turkey. They were arrested and sentenced to 10 years in Special Political prison camps. Roman was sent to Norylsk Gulag where he took an active part in prisoners' uprising in the summer of 1953. Roman's co-defendants Vitaly Svechinsky and Mikhail Margulis were sent to other Siberian camps. All of them survived five years imprisonment and were released in 1955 in the first post-Stalin amnesty. In 1959 Roman managed to leave the Soviet Union legally - his wife was a Polish citizen. In 1962 he, his wife and their two sons immigrated to the United States. In 1965 Roman graduated from City College of New York with bachelor degree in science and in 1980 he received the doctorate degree in history from New York University. During Carter-Reagan election campaign in 1979-1980 Roman published his first book "Jimmy Carter Provocateur-in-Chief." His book "The Secret File of Joseph Stalin - A Hidden Life" was published in 2001 in London and translated to several languages, including Russian. His book "Israel at High Noon" was published in 2006 in New York. In 2010 Roman published "Watergate and Deep Throat Hoax" - a book about Nixon Presidency during the Watergate scandal and the role played by John Dean. His book "First Jewish President", published in 2012, examines the support extended by Chicago Jewish community to the young unknown politician Barack Obama.